GEORGE EDWARD MOORE

1873–1958

GEORGE EDWARD MOORE was born on 4 November 1873 at Upper Norwood, London. His father, Daniel Moore, M.D., had been in general practice as a doctor at Hastings; but being a man of private means he had moved to London, and ceased to practise, a year or two before G. E. Moore was born.

Daniel Moore's father, George Moore (1803–80; in *D.N.B.*), had also practised medicine, and had been the author of several successful books on what would now be called 'popular philosophy'. Moore's mother, Henrietta Sturge, was the daughter of two first cousins, both Sturges and members of that well-known Quaker family. Joseph Sturge the philanthropist (1793–1859; in *D.N.B.*) was her uncle. Moore was the fifth child in a family of eight, four boys and four girls; so the recently built red-brick house at Upper Norwood, with half an acre of garden, on the western slope of the hill rising to where was then the Crystal Palace, contained, as Moore has said, 'enough of us to make plenty of company for one another'. His eldest brother, Thomas Sturge Moore, the poet, artist, and critic, had a great influence on the formation of his opinions: Moore attributed to him a large share of responsibility for the falling away of his religious beliefs before he had left school. (The Moore parents were Baptists.) In the very characteristic thirty-nine-page 'Autobiography' which Moore wrote to prefix to the collection of articles in *The Philosophy of G. E. Moore* (ed. P. A. Schilpp: 1942) [referred to as *PGEM*], he makes no reference to the characters of his parents; but he leaves no doubt that he had a happy childhood, both at home and at school.

One of the reasons for the Moore family moving to Upper Norwood was that the sons should be able to be day boys at Dulwich College under its great first headmaster A. H. Gilkes. Moore went there at the age of 8, and stayed there for ten years and two terms, walking (or running) the mile between home and school four times four days of the week and twice on Wednesdays and Saturdays. The account Moore has given of his formal education there will curdle the blood of any modern educationalist devoted to the cause of a balanced education. Moore was good at classics and went up the school rapidly on the 'classical side', and his last six years (*aet.* 12¾–18½) were spent in the top two forms where almost all his time was devoted to Greek and Latin, mostly to translation into these languages in prose or verse. Moore never regretted this concentration upon classics: he said that the variety of English passages which he was required to translate made him appreciate their qualities. Though Moore learned little mathematics and no science, he was well grounded in German; and the head of the musical department (E. D. Rendall) gave him private lessons in singing and introduced him to Schubert's and other *Lieder*, which later Moore used to sing, accompanying himself on the piano, to the great delight of his friends.

It is evident from Moore's account that his enjoyment of the Sixth Form at Dulwich was largely due to two great teachers— W. T. Lendrum, who later became a Fellow of Caius College, Cambridge (and changed his name to Vesey), and the headmaster, A. H. Gilkes. Moore's portrait of Gilkes (*PGEM*, 9) compares him to the Platonic Socrates: the talks he gave to the Sixth Form in their weekly classes with him, and the essays which they wrote for him on the 'astounding variety of different subjects' of these talks, must have provided in themselves a liberal education.

It is not surprising that when Moore went up to Trinity College, Cambridge, in October 1892 (with a Major Entrance Scholarship) to read for Part I of the Classical Tripos, he found that the work to be done during his first two years at Cambridge largely repeated what he had done at Dulwich. Moore profited in these years by forming, for the first time, 'intimate friendships with extremely clever people.... Until I went to Cambridge, I had had no idea how exciting life could be' (*PGEM*, 13). Many of these men were a year or two his senior, and Moore was surprised that they should make friends with him. But if they impressed Moore by their brilliance combined with 'very great seriousness', there is no doubt of the remarkable impression which Moore made upon them. Bertrand Russell has written:

In my third year I met G. E. Moore, who was then a freshman, and for some years he fulfilled my ideal of genius. He was in those days beautiful and slim, with a look almost of inspiration, and with an intellect as deeply passionate as Spinoza's. He had a kind of exquisite purity [*Portraits from Memory and other Essays*, 1956, p. 68].

Russell introduced him to J. E. McTaggart, then a young Fellow of Trinity; and Moore believed that it was the way he held his own in argument with McTaggart at their first meeting which made Russell think that he had 'some aptitude for philosophy' and encourage him to read moral science in his third year.

Many of Moore's friends were members of the 'Apostles' discussion society; and Moore was elected to this in his second year. This Society played a large part in Moore's life during his first period in Cambridge (and till quite late in life he attended its meetings on special occasions); and Moore played a leading part in the Society. Leonard Woolf, describing in his recent autobiography the Society as he knew it in 1901, has written:

> Throughout its history, every now and again an Apostle has dominated and left his impression, within its spirit and tradition, upon the Society. Sidgwick was one of these, and a century ago he dominated the Society, refertilizing and revivifying its spirit and tradition. And what Sidgwick did in the fifties of last century, G. E. Moore was doing when I was elected [*Sowing*, 1960, p. 130].

Further testimony to the influence at this time of Moore's 'combination of clarity, integrity, tenacity, and passion' (Woolf's words) will be found in the biographies of G. Lowes Dickinson by E. M. Forster (p. 110) and of J. M. Keynes by R. F. Harrod (p. 75). And those of us who knew Moore twenty years later would not have written differently.

To go back to 1894. Moore got his First that year in Part I of the Classical Tripos (and won the University Craven Scholarship in January 1895) and took to philosophy. In his Autobiography he records his debt to four of his teachers, James Ward, G. F. Stout, McTaggart (lecturing on Hegel), and Henry Jackson (lecturing on Plato and Aristotle, for Moore was simultaneously reading Ancient Philosophy for the Classical Part II). After obtaining a First, with a mark of distinction, in Part II of the Moral Sciences Tripos in 1896 (and in the same month a Second in Part II Classics), he worked for a Trinity Fellowship, submitting a dissertation on 'Freedom' in 1897. He added a concluding chapter on 'Reason' for the annual election of 1898, when he was elected to what was then called a 'Prize' fellowship with a tenure of six years. Thus Moore had full freedom to develop his philosophical ideas 'living in a set of Fellows' rooms on the north side of Nevile's Court—a very pleasant place and a very pleasant life'. Moore reported in 1942 that he did a respectable, 'but, I am afraid, not more than respectable', amount of work (and he went on to explain how lazy he was by nature: *PGEM*, 24–5). Since in these six years Moore published, besides many articles in philosophical journals and in Baldwin's *Dictionary of Philosophy*, the book which made his philosophical reputation, *Principia Ethica* (1903), 'magnificent' would seem a more appropriate epithet to apply to Moore's performance as a prize fellow.

Moore's philosophical teachers (except Sidgwick) were all, one way or another, philosophical Idealists; and Moore, like Russell, started his philosophizing as a Bradleyan–Hegelian Idealist. (F. H. Bradley's *Appearance and Reality* had appeared in 1893.) Moore's first published writing was a contribution to an Aristotelian Society symposium on the sense in which past and future time exist: he concluded it by saying: 'Time must be rejected wholly, its continuity as well as its discreteness, if we are to form an adequate notion of reality . . . neither Past, Present, nor Future exists, if by existence we are to mean the ascription of full Reality and not merely existence as Appearance' (*Mind*, vi, 1897, p. 240). And a few months later, 'the arguments by which Mr. Bradley has endeavoured to prove the unreality of Time appear to me perfectly conclusive' (*Mind*, vii, 1898, p. 202). When twenty years later Moore tore these conclusions to pieces (*Philosophical Studies*, 1922 [*PS*], chap. vi), he was making amends for the sins of his youth. However, Moore passed out of his Idealist phase very quickly, carrying Russell along with him. The Aristotelian Society paper 'The Nature of Judgement' (*Mind*, viii, 1899, pp. 176 ff.), developed out of Moore's second fellowship dissertation, shows him insisting, in opposition to Bradley, that fact is independent of experience. From the end of 1898 Moore separated himself completely from the dominant Idealist school, and his famous 1903 *Mind* article entitled 'The Refutation of Idealism' (*PS*, chap. i) directly attacked the proposition, 'essential to Idealism', that *esse* is *percipi*.

The ethical system which Moore expounded in *Principia Ethica* [*PE*] is firmly rooted in his philosophical Realism. Just as yellowness is a simple unanalysable property of things in the world so also is goodness. This thesis of the unanalysability of goodness has been regarded by professional philosophers for the last thirty years as the most important part of the book; but for his Cambridge friends what came as a revelation was the combination of this thesis with the insistence that there are many different sorts of things which are good in themselves ('worth having *purely for their own sakes*'), by 'far the most valuable' of which are 'certain states of consciousness, which may be roughly described as the pleasures of human intercourse and the enjoyment of beautiful objects' (*PE*, 188). J. M. Keynes (*Two Memoirs*, 1949, pp. 81 ff.) and Leonard Woolf (*Sowing*, pp. 144 ff.)

have given fascinating accounts of the impact of *Principia Ethica* upon the Cambridge intellectuals of the time. The considerable difference between their two accounts may arise partly from the fact that each had attached most importance to that in it which spoke to his own condition. What spoke to the condition of my generation in the immediate post-First-World-War period, when *Principia Ethica* was as widely read by intelligent undergraduates as ever before, was its non-hedonistic and pluralistic utilitarianism ('Ideal Utilitarianism', as W. D. Ross later called it); and we would have agreed with Leonard Woolf that

Moore's distinction between things good in themselves or as ends and things good merely as means, his passionate search for truth in his attempt in *Principia Ethica* to determine what things are good in themselves, answered our questions, not with the religious voice of Jehovah from Mount Sinai or Jesus with his Sermon from the Mount [nor, we would have added, with the authoritarian voice of the State telling us what it was our duty to do], but with the more divine voice of plain common-sense [p. 148].

When Moore's prize fellowship at Trinity ran out in 1904, the recent death of both his parents had left him with some private means; and he went to live at Edinburgh, sharing an apartment in Buccleuch Place with his friend A. R. Ainsworth who held a lectureship at Edinburgh University. In 1908 Moore moved south to set up house with two of his sisters on the Green at Richmond, Surrey; and in 1911 he returned to Cambridge on his appointment to a university lectureship there. Except for four years in America during the Second World War the rest of his life was spent in Cambridge.

Moore said that during these seven years away from Cambridge he 'worked at philosophy as hard as, though no harder than' he had worked during the six years of his fellowship. Besides writing the book *Ethics* for the Home University Library series (1912) and articles on William James's pragmatism and Hume's philosophy, he started on a line of thought about the philosophical problems of perception which he continued all the rest of his life and which, by his Cambridge lectures as well as by his published writings, has profoundly influenced Anglo-American philosophy. Moore centred his discussion upon the notion of things which are 'directly apprehended' in sense-perception, which he first called 'sense-contents' (*PS*, 79) but later 'sense-data'. This was the term which Moore used in the lectures he wrote out for delivery at Morley College in London in 1910: although these lectures were not published until 1953 (under the title of *Some Main Problems of Philosophy* [*SMPP*], see p. 30), Russell had read this part of the manuscript when, in his Home University Library volume *The Problems of Philosophy* (1912), he gave wide publicity to the term and notion of 'sense-datum'.

For Moore the fundamental question in the philosophy of perception was the relation of these sense-data to material objects. In the six pages devoted to this problem in the famous article 'A Defence of Common Sense' which he contributed to *Contemporary British Philosophy* (second series: ed. J. H. Muirhead) in 1925 (reprinted in *Philosophical Papers*, 1959 [*PP*]), Moore gave three possible types of answer to the question: what do I know about a visual sense-datum when I know that it is a sense-datum of my hand? The first answer was that I know that the sense-datum is part of the surface of my hand (*direct realism*). The second type of answer (*representativism*) was that what I know is that there is a unique part of the surface of my hand which stands in an 'ultimate relation' R to the sense-datum. The third type (*phenomenalism*) was that all that I know is a whole set of hypothetical facts to the effect that, if certain conditions had held, I should have perceived other sense-data intrinsically related in certain ways to this sense-datum. [The type-names in italics are mine.]

Consideration of the arguments for and against answers of these three types frequently took up the whole year (forty or sixty lectures) of one of Moore's lecture courses at Cambridge in the twenties. Besides discussing answers of the different types put forward by various philosophers (after first elucidating exactly what it was they wanted to say), Moore invented several forms of answer which were less open to objection. Hardly any of these highly original philosophic-theory-construction analyses are to be found in Moore's own publications, though some of them found their way, with due acknowledgement, into the justly celebrated writings of philosophers who had sat at his feet.

One reason why Moore, in his prime of life, never wrote a book on perception (or indeed on anything else) is, I suspect, that he saw the reasons against any view so clearly that he could never make up his mind which was on the whole the most defensible, especially since he was ingenious in recasting every theory into its least objectionable form. More of his thinking about direct realism—that the visual sense-data which we directly see are parts of surfaces of material objects—survives in his published writings than of his thinking about representativism or about phenomenalism (which is only discussed in some ten pages: *SMPP*, 132–5; *PS*, 188–92, 250–1; *PP*, 57–58). Perhaps because of this some present-day direct realists have claimed him as their master. I have no doubt at all that Moore would have liked to be a direct realist if his intellectual conscience had permitted him. But after sitting on the fence for forty years he definitely decided against direct realism in his last paper ('Visual Sense-Data', in *British Philosophy in the Mid-Century*, ed. C. A. Mace, 1957). Moore left no indication as to which of the other views he would prefer; but in his Cambridge lectures in the middle thirties phenomenalism received a far more favourable treatment than might have been expected.

Moore never lectured on ethics in Cambridge, and the developments of his ethical theory since *Principia Ethica* are to be found in his published writings. In *Principia Ethica* he had taken the goodness of the consequences of an action as defining the 'rightness' of the action; but in subsequent works he regarded rightness and goodness as independently given notions interrelated by logical relations. The only one of his later ethical writings which breaks really new ground is the ethical part of his 'Reply to My Critics' (*PGEM*, 535 ff.). Here among other things he discusses the 'emotive' theory of ethics, as it was then called, which had been put forward by C. L. Stevenson in his criticism of Moore, according to which the essential function of an ethical statement lies in its *emotive* and not in its *cognitive* meaning. Moore, indeed, goes further than Stevenson in suggesting that an ethical statement might have no cognitive meaning whatever ('nothing whatever that could possibly be true or false'). This view Moore admitted would be paradoxical, but he thought that 'very possibly it may be true' (*PGEM*, 542). Indeed at the end of his discussion he says that he is both inclined to think that ethical words have merely emotive meaning and inclined to think the contrary, and 'I do not know which way I am inclined most strongly' (*PGEM*, 554). It is rare to find a philosopher open-minded enough to be prepared, in his sixty-ninth year, to speak in this manner of a view which cuts away the presupposition of a doctrine that had made him famous in his youth and that he had maintained all his life.

When Moore returned to Cambridge in 1911 as University Lecturer in Moral Science, it was arranged, to suit the teaching requirements, that he should give the lectures on Psychology for Part I of the Tripos. But, as is the Cambridge practice, the lecturer was given pretty complete freedom in deciding how to treat his subject. Moore has described how, influenced by the fact that C. S. Myers was giving lectures on Experimental Psychology, he designed his course as one on the Philosophy of Mind. He gave this course, three times a week throughout the three terms, for fourteen years. But from 1918 onwards he also lectured on Metaphysics, at least twice a week until 1925 (when he succeeded James Ward in his professorship) and three times a week after that until his retirement in 1939. Moore held discussion classes in connexion with each of his courses, and frequently it happened that a point raised in discussion made him revise in his next lecture what he had previously said. Moore never took sabbatical leave, and very seldom missed a lecture through illness; so any philosopher wishing to know how Moore was thinking could rely on finding him in Cambridge lecturing three times a week. Particularly after 1925, when 'A Defence of Common Sense' caused rumours of his 'method of analysis' to spread throughout the English-speaking philosophical world, there was hardly a year in which there were not one or two British or American philosophers, junior and senior, who had contrived, sometimes with great difficulty, to spend a term or a year in Cambridge to sit at Moore's feet.

Whatever the subject-matter or nominal title of the lectures, examples of philosophic analyses were what Moore provided. In 'A Defence of Common Sense' Moore insisted, with respect to an unambiguous expression (like 'The earth has existed for many years past'), that 'the question whether we understand its meaning (which we all certainly do)' must be distinguished from 'the entirely different question whether we *know what it means*, in the sense that we are able to *give a correct analysis* of its meaning' (*PP*, 37). Moore's lectures were searches for correct analyses. One possible analysis was propounded, and elucidated in great detail; it was found defective in various ways, but could be modified to avoid these defects. But then the modifications had other defects. After worrying at and improving one type of analysis throughout some twenty lectures, Moore would then pass to another possible type and repeat the process of elucidating, criticizing, modifying, and criticizing again. In 1922–3, when I attended both courses of Moore's lectures, we hunted the correct analysis of propositions about the self on Monday, Wednesday, and Friday mornings and the correct analysis of propositions of the form 'This is a pencil' on Tuesday, Thursday, and Saturday mornings throughout the year. By the end of May, when lectures had to stop because the triposes started, Moore would have got through about two-and-a-half of the possible kinds of analysis. The lectures were quite inconclusive: Moore saw grave objections to any of the analyses he had discussed being the *correct* analysis, and the audience dispersed to sit their examinations, or to return to their homes across the Atlantic, without any idea as to which of the analyses had the best claim to correctness. Of course Moore was concealing nothing: he himself did not know which solution to prefer. In his 'Reply to My Critics', where he commented upon L. S. Stebbing's defence of him against Rudolf Metz's judgement that 'though we may call Moore the greatest, acutest and most skilful questioner of modern philosophy, we must add that he is an extremely weak and unsatisfying answerer' *(PGEM*, 521), he said: 'I did want to answer questions, to give solutions to problems, and I think it is a just charge against me that I have been able to solve so few of the problems I wished to solve.' And he added that he thought that probably one of the reasons for this was that he had 'not gone about the business of trying to solve them the right way' *(PGEM*, 677).

The way in which he went about trying to solve these problems was the way of 'analysis'; but Moore rarely directly attacked the question of what it is to give an analysis, and there are only eight pages in his published writings devoted explicitly to this question *(PGEM*, 660–7). Here he is concerned with the analysis of a concept (e.g. being a brother) and the analysis of a proposition (e.g. John is a brother); and from the examples of analysanda which Moore always takes in other places it is clear that he regarded an analysis of a proposition as the fundamental notion in terms of which the analysis of a concept was to be explained. For the purpose of analysis a concept cannot be treated in isolation: it must be considered in the contexts of the propositions in which it can occur. In lectures (which I attended) given in Cambridge in 1933–4, Moore went further than this: he said that sometimes a proposition cannot be analysed in isolation, but must be considered in relation to propositions which are its logical consequences. Here the system of logically related propositions would be the fundamental unit for analysis, and the analysis of the proposition would be given by means of its logical relations to propositions whose analysis was of a different kind. In mentioning this possibility Moore may perhaps have been influenced by F. P. Ramsey's ideas on the understanding of 'Theories', posthumously published in 1931 in a book to which Moore wrote a preface. Certainly what Moore was here suggesting, and the emphasis throughout his lectures on the relevance to analysing a proposition of what are its logical consequences, was in line with some of the things that Rudolf Carnap was about to say in his *Logische Syntax der Sprache* (1934). When I lectured on this book a few years later, I was able to make Carnap's way of thinking appear less alien to Cambridge philosophers by pointing out similarities to what Moore had been saying in an entirely different manner.

I have tried to indicate how it was that those of us who sat at Moore's feet regarded him as a far more original thinker, and one whose thought was always developing more, than did those whose knowledge of him was confined to his published writings. During the twenty-eight years of his teaching life at Cambridge Moore's conscientiousness in preparing his lectures, which were never the same from year to year, and his editorship after 1921 of *Mind*, left him little time for writing for publication. Almost all he published during this period were contributions to symposia at the Joint Sessions of the Aristotelian Society and the Mind Association, where Moore did what he was asked to do by discussing and criticizing most lucidly what had been said by other philosophers, but rarely added any ideas of his own. The great exception is 'A Defence of Common Sense' to which I have frequently referred (since for me it is the work most characteristic of Moore at the height of his powers); but this article only whets the appetite for a meal which the cook appears to be saving for his Cambridge *clientèle*. To use contemporary jargon, the public 'image' which Moore presents to many of his readers—that of a modern Johnson refuting the modern Berkeleys by holding up his hands instead of kicking a stone—is quite different from that of a philosopher with subtle and original ideas upon a great variety of important philosophical issues which is the 'image' that his pupils in the twenties and thirties formed of him. To give some examples from my own experience, Moore produced for us original ideas on causal theories of perception, on the analysis of 'If . . . then . . .' propositions, on the 'incomplete symbols' of *Principia Mathematica*, on how one gets to know logical truths, on the relations of expressions to one another and to what they mean (and the inter-relationships of these various relations), on the importance of criteria of identity in giving analyses. Frequently, when I read excellent books and articles by distinguished contemporary philosophers, I find points which I remember hearing from Moore. [Indeed one of Moore's earliest publications contains the argument that 'in virtue of the deterministic hypothesis itself, the knowledge that a certain course of action was about to be pursued must always . . . make the result different from what was foreseen after a consideration of all the other elements that would contribute to it' and hence that 'the results of human volition, alone among causes, must *of necessity* remain incapable of prediction' (*Mind*, vii, 1898, p. 187), an argument which has been very prominent in recent free-will discussions, where it is usually attributed to an unpublished paper by Gilbert Ryle in the thirties.] After Moore's death there was found among his papers a 'Commonplace Book' in which he had recorded ideas for his private use: a selection of these entries is being prepared by Casimir Lewy for publication and will, I hope, show the wide variety of the questions with which Moore was concerned.

The main feature in the public image of Moore is his appeal to 'common sense' in his refutation of what Hume called 'excessive scepticism'; but how this appeal should be understood has been the subject recently of fierce controversy. In 'A Defence of Common Sense' Moore, after giving examples of propositions such as 'My own and many other human bodies live on the earth' which are fundamental features of the 'Common Sense view of the world', says that 'I am one of those philosophers who have held that the "Common Sense view of the world" is, in certain fundamental features, *wholly* true'. And he goes on to say: 'According to me, *all* philosophers, without exception, have agreed with me in holding this: . . the real difference . . . is only a difference between those philosophers, who have *also* held views inconsistent with these features in "the Common Sense view of the world", and those who have not' (*PP*, 44). This would seem to be clear enough. But several commentators on Moore have thought that he could not be speaking literally when he spoke of philosophers who held 'sincerely, as part of their philosophical creed, propositions inconsistent with what they themselves *knew* to be true' (*PP*, 41), since it is impossible for philosophers to hold views which they know to be false (Morris Lazerowitz, *PGEM*, 380). These commentators have therefore wished to say that what is important in Moore's argument is his pointing out that philosophers who make statements which appear to contradict common sense are using words in ways which deviate from the ordinary use of language. Norman Malcolm, for example, regards Moore's 'so-called defence of Common Sense, in so far as it is an interesting and tenable philosophical position', as being 'merely the assertion, in regard to various sentences, that those sentences have a correct use in ordinary language' (*Mind*, lxix, 1960, p. 97). Malcolm adds: 'This makes it into a very simple idea, but that is what good ideas sometimes are.'

But what Moore was concerned with was an even simpler and better idea—that philosophers ought not to contradict themselves. As Moore said in 1942, in reply to Lazerowitz, 'there is no reason whatever to suppose that this is impossible' (*PGEM*, 675), and, in a similar connexion in 1903, 'it is very easy to hold two mutually contradictory opinions' (*PS*, 13). And Moore knew what he was talking about, for in his early short Bradleyan phase he had indulged in exactly that type of 'double thinking' which he was to castigate in his maturity. Moore's anti-sceptical protest was directed against the temptation to which every philosopher (and linguistic philosopher) is subject, to be carried away by the apparent self-evidence of his premisses or cogency of his argumentation into believing ridiculous conclusions—ridiculous because they contradict those common-sense beliefs which he has no intention of discarding. Hume oscillated between the 'philosophical melancholy and delirium' of 'excessive scepticism' and being merry playing backgammon with his friends. Moore rejected such a double life: the backgammon player, while philosophizing, must never forget that he continues to hold his common-sense beliefs. Moore's attack on the inconsistency of double thinking was as much moral as intellectual; and G. J. Warnock has rightly emphasized the influence upon philosophy of 'the *character* of G. E. Moore' (*English Philosophy since 1900*, 1958, pp. 11–12).

In his Autobiography Moore mentions the works of Bertrand Russell, W. E. Johnson, and C. D. Broad as those which had provided points upon which he had lectured in detail, and Johnson and F. P. Ramsey as those with whom he had long discussions on philosophy. Moore saw a good deal of Ludwig Wittgenstein in 1912–14, and after 1929 attended many courses of his lectures, 'always with admiration': after Wittgenstein's death he published an account of the contents of courses which he had attended between 1930 and 1933 (*PP*, 252–324). 'How far he has influenced positively anything that I have written, I cannot tell', Moore wrote in 1942. (My own view is that no positive influence is detectable.) But Wittgenstein made him 'very distrustful about many things which, but for him, I should have been inclined to assert positively' and 'think that what is required for the solution of philosophical problems which baffle me, is a method quite different from any which I have ever used —a method which he himself uses successfully' (*PGEM*, 33). Moore never attempted to employ Wittgenstein's or any other method of 'linguistic philosophy'; in his lectures in the thirties he discussed at length relations between synonymous expressions, but this was always in connexion with the analyses of the concepts or propositions for which these expressions stood. If, as some present-day philosophers suggest, Moore's anti-scepticism and method of analysis will take their place in the history of philosophy as *intimations* of a philosophy grounded on considerations as to how language is used, they will only be intimations in a Wordsworthian sense. For me Moore marks the end of one epoch rather than the beginning of another, though I should agree that the new epoch could hardly have begun if Moore had not definitively refuted the 'excessive scepticism' which has been such a temptation to post-Cartesian philosophers.

I have devoted so much space in this memoir to Moore's philosophical thinking partly because it has been misunderstood, partly because Moore's published writings do not display his full originality, but chiefly because, in his public character, Moore was a philosopher and nothing but a philosopher. In this is included being an educator of philosophers: Moore's single-minded and passionate devotion to the search for truth inspired all who came into contact with him. Moore was no respecter of persons. In the discussions following his lectures, at the weekly meetings of the Cambridge Moral Science Club which Moore regularly attended, and at the Joint Sessions of the Aristotelian Society and the Mind Association held annually at different universities, the beginner in philosophy who ventured with trepidation to raise a difficulty would find Moore assisting him to put his point more clearly, while a scholar of world-wide renown might find Moore telling him that he was talking utter nonsense. Moore's interventions were accompanied by gestures of his pipe and his whole body and with characteristically over-emphasized words ('*Oh!* you *really* think *that?*') which made it impossible for anyone to take offence. Moore's mere presence raised the tone of a philosophical discussion: it made flippancy or sarcasm or bombast impossible. We were compelled, sometimes against our wills, to be as serious, and to try to be as sincere, as Moore so obviously was himself.

Moore's endearing directness and simplicity showed itself also in university committees; and I will give two characteristic examples which continue to give me great pleasure. The first occurred in 1929 when Wittgenstein, returned to Cambridge, submitted his *Tractatus Logico-Philosophicus* as his Ph.D. dissertation. Russell and Moore were appointed his examiners; and Moore's written report to the Moral Science Degree Committee concluded as follows (I quote from memory): 'I myself consider that this is a work of genius; but, even if I am completely mistaken and it is nothing of the sort, it is well above the standard required for the Ph.D. degree.'

The second example concerns the title of the Chair which Moore occupied. When Moore was elected to it in 1925 it was the Professorship of Mental Philosophy and Logic, a title doubtless chosen in 1896 to give free scope to its first holder, James Ward. In 1933 the Council of the Senate thought that difficulties might be presented to the electors in the many cases of Cambridge chairs which had conjunctive titles, and asked the Faculty Board of Moral Science to consider omitting the reference to Logic in the title of the Chair so that the two philosophical chairs would be respectively of Mental Philosophy and of Moral Philosophy (the latter being the seventeenth-century Knightbridge Chair then held by C. D. Broad). We on the Faculty Board did not wish to perpetuate the obsolescent term 'Mental Philosophy', particularly since a Professorship of Experimental Psychology had recently been established; and we had a high philosophic discussion as to the best titles for the two chairs. Moore proposed that his Chair should be called that of *Theoretical* Philosophy and the Knightbridge Chair that of *Practical* Philosophy, citing Sidgwick as the authority for this dichotomy. We took a lot of time persuading Moore that such titles would give rise to ribaldry at our expense, for his proposal seemed to him so sweetly reasonable. Finally it was settled that the Knightbridge Chair should continue to be that of Moral Philosophy, but that Moore's chair should be the Professorship of Philosophy with no qualifying adjective.

Moore had at different times been Secretary and Chairman of the Faculty Board of Moral Science, and for four years (1933–6) he was a member of the General Board of the Faculties as one of the two representatives of the group of four faculties which included Moral Science. Moore was no innovator in university matters, though he was open-minded to reforms suggested by others. His strength in council was his judicial cast of mind; and he was an excellent examiner and writer of testimonials. When he became professor in 1925 he was re-elected a Fellow of Trinity (as a Professorial Fellow); and he served a four-year term as a member of the Trinity College Council. But he is most remembered in Trinity for *Die beiden Grenadiere*, which he sang each year at the party following the Commemoration Feast.

In 1921 Moore succeeded G. F. Stout as editor of *Mind*, and the twenty-six years of his editorship enhanced the high reputation of that journal. Moore took enormous trouble in corresponding, in his own hand, with contributors and in suggesting improvements in exposition; many young philosophers are deeply grateful to him for the informal 'tutorials' they thus received. The co-operation of Lewy in Cambridge enabled him to continue being editor through the years 1940–4 when he was in America; but increasing infirmity compelled him to resign in 1947.

Moore took a Cambridge Litt.D. degree in 1913, and in 1918 was given an Honorary LL.D. by St. Andrews and elected a Fellow of the British Academy. He was President of the Aristotelian Society for the year 1918–19. In June of 1951 he was appointed to the Order of Merit. By a fortunate coincidence the Cambridge Vice-Chancellor was giving a garden party in Pembroke for the benefit of the recipients of honorary degrees, on the day on which the Honours List was published. It was a brilliantly fine afternoon; and Moore (*aet.* 77) was able to attend, and to sit in a chair to receive our congratulations and to learn (if he did not know it before) how much we all respected and loved him.

In 1915–16 Moore made the acquaintance of Dorothy Ely, a Newnham graduate who was attending his lectures in her fourth year; and they were married in December 1916. They first lived in a flat at 17 Magdalene Street, nearly opposite Magdalene College. Two sons were born of the marriage, and Moore became a devoted family man. In the early twenties one would meet him any fine afternoon pushing a perambulator along the Backs. In 1922 the Moores moved to a semi-detached house, 86 Chesterton Road, about three-quarters of a mile from the centre of the town, which was to be their home for the rest of his life. All visitors to the house were received with an easy welcome; and one of the pleasures of being a Tripos examiner with Moore as chairman was that we met at 86 Chesterton Road and, when our morning's business was concluded, we descended into the semi-basement for a delicious luncheon, ending with glasses of Canary sack. It is impertinent to comment on happy marriages: all that I shall say is that the Moores provided a model of a way of living in which simplicity and seriousness were combined with an extroverted enjoyment of the good things of life.

In September 1939 Moore retired from his Cambridge Chair, having reached the age of 65. He became Emeritus Professor of Philosophy and remained a Fellow of Trinity. During the Michaelmas Term of 1939 he went over once a week to Oxford to lecture—to a larger audience, as he reports, than had ever attended his lectures before. In August 1940 his American friends and former pupils Alice Ambrose and Morris Lazerowitz thought it better that he should think and teach philosophy in the United States than assist, at his age, in the Battle of Britain; and he was invited to be Neilson Visiting Professor at Smith College in Massachusetts for the autumn semester. He and his wife arrived in America in October and stayed there until May 1944. During the spring of 1941 he lectured at Princeton; and in the summer Moore went west to be Howison Lecturer at the University of California in Berkeley, living (and also teaching) at Mills College near San Francisco. During this year Moore was largely occupied in writing the 145-page 'Reply to My Critics' (in *PGEM*), the most substantial and important work of his later life. At the end of the year the Moores returned to the eastern states; and Moore lived in New York and taught at Columbia University for two consecutive semesters in 1942 and throughout the academical year 1943–4. During the spring of 1943 he lectured at Swarthmore College in Pennsylvania. Moore gave single lectures at many other universities, and the Moores were able to visit their American friends during vacations. Moore had never been to the United States before, and was deeply appreciative of the kindness shown to him and Mrs. Moore in these difficult years. From the American side Morton White (who had not sat at Moore's feet in Cambridge) has testified to the great impression Moore made upon the young New York philosophers. 'I believe that Moore, more than any of his distinguished contemporaries, communicated to his students the feeling that they could share his method even when they did not accept his philosophical beliefs.' ' "Do your philosophy for yourself" . . . was one of Moore's great messages to the young' (*The Journal of Philosophy*, lvii, 1960, p. 807).

Moore had had a few illnesses in America; and on his return to Cambridge in 1944 his doctor, to our great disappointment, forbade him the over-excitement that would result from his taking part in discussions at the Moral Science Club. For the rest of his life Moore rarely appeared in public, though he was

able for some years to dine weekly in Trinity. He gave great
pleasure to a group of European philosophers by appearing for
an informal discussion about sense-data at a symposium organ-
ized for them at Peterhouse in 1953 by the British Council; and
he wrote the short paper 'Visual Sense-Data' (already men-
tioned) specially for the volume that arose out of the symposium.
Up to the end of his life he was able to talk philosophy for
limited periods with individual friends, particularly Casimir
Lewy and John Wisdom. But he was gradually getting feebler,
and for the last few years osteoarthritis confined him to his house,
though not to his bed. In the summer of 1958 he had to go into
Addenbrooke's Hospital with a painful illness; and he died in
Cambridge on 24 October eleven days before his eighty-fifth
birthday.

R. B. BRAITHWAITE

[NOTE ADDED IN PROOF.] On p. 299 I have quoted Moore's confession
in his last publication on ethics (1942), that, with regard to his rival
inclinations to think that ethical words have merely emotive meaning
and to think the contrary, 'I do not know which way I am inclined most
strongly' (PGEM, 554). A. C. Ewing has recently reported that, in
a conversation he had with Moore at some date after 1953, Moore said
that 'he still held to his old view [that ethical statements have cognitive
meaning], and further that he could not imagine whatever in the world
had induced him to say that he was almost equally inclined to hold the
other view' (Mind, lxxi, 1962, p. 251).   R. B. B.

PLATE XLIX

Photograph by N. Moore, 1954

GEORGE EDWARD MOORE, O.M.

Date Due

CPSIA information can be obtained
at www.ICGtesting.com
Printed in the USA
BVHW021929120223
658261BV00022BA/60